LOW CARBS HIGH PROTEIN

MUSCLE- BUILDING

MEAL PREP

COOKBOOK

A Complete Macro Guide with Yummy, Easy And Delicious High Protein Low Carb Diet Recipes For Burning Fat , Building Muscles and Getting Lean

Theresa Lynch

All rights reserved, No part of this publication should be reprinted or transmitted through electronic mechanical means without prior permission by the Author, except for citations for critical uses.

Copyright Theresa Lynch, 2022

Table of contents

Body Building & Nutrition
    Prioritize protein

Main Recipes
    Spinach Tomato Frittata
    High-Protein Veggie Egg
    Chicken in Air Fryer
    Shrimp, Avocado, and Egg Chopped Salad
    Rotisserie Chicken Salad Recipe
    Pan Seared Chicken Breast Recipe
    Salmon Meal Prep With Veggies (High Protein)
    Stir-Fried Pork Meal Prep With Ginger and Soy
    Sheet Pan Italian Sausage and Pepper Bake
    Chicken With Fried Cauliflower Rice
    Moroccan Eggs with Harissa Yogurt
    Roasted Chicken and Potatoes With Kale
    White Wine and Tomato Mussels
    Baked Salmon with Roasted Red Pepper Sauce
    Roasted Shrimp Parmesan
    Honey Lime Air Fryer Shrimp
    Baked Chicken Nuggets
    Beef and Broccoli
    Slow Cooker Beef Chile Verde
    Salsa Shredded Chicken
    Egg Salad Bowls
    Mexican Meal Prep Bowls with Cauliflower Rice

Turkey Kebabs
Broiled Beef Shish Kebabsi
Air Fryer Chicken Drumsticks
Spinach Egg Bake
Air Fryer Cod
Salmon Croquette
Lamb Shish Kebab
Greek Sheet Pan Chicken
Low Carb Greek Chicken
Instant Pot Salmon with Frozen Fillets
Protein Snack Pack
Protein Pancakes
Protein Waffles

Body Building & Nutrition

Bodybuilders, trainers and diet gurus alike (at least those worth their salt) will tell you that bodybuilding is more than 50% nutrition.

We tend to agree, especially where the novice is concerned. Beginners or anyone returning to the gym after a break might expect to see significant increases in strength and bulk with a regular training regimen, but only with a well-rounded eating plan.

Your gains will be more significant the more seriously you take nutrition. In fact, if you looked through the weightlifting literature, you'd find that there are a lot more studies on the effects of diet and nutritional supplements than there are on training methods for increasing muscle development and strength. According to the research, paying attention to calories, meal timing, macronutrients (protein, carbs, and fat), and certain supplements will have a significant impact on your results.

Prioritize protein

Daily protein intake should be at least 1 gram per pound of body weight. Amino acids, which serve as the building blocks of muscle protein, are provided by protein.

Although the average person's recommended daily protein intake is less than half a gram per pound of bodyweight, research indicates that athletes, particularly those concerned with muscle building and strength, require nearly twice that amount daily.

For the first six months of exercise, beginners should actually aim to consume 1.5 grams of protein per pound of bodyweight each day because this is when your muscles will react to training the fastest. This translates to 270 grams per day at first and a bare minimum of 180 grams per day thereafter for the 180-pounder.

Lean animal proteins like chicken, turkey, beef, fish, eggs, and dairy products should make up the majority of your protein selections. These protein sources are the most comprehensive since they give your body all of the essential amino acids, which are those that it cannot produce on its own.

Your daily caloric intake should contain 20%–30% of fat. Furthermore, 5%–10% of your fat calories should be saturated, as opposed to the advice given to the sedentary general population, as higher-fat diets (especially those higher in monounsaturated and saturated fats) appear to maintain testosterone levels better than low-fat diets.

Low Carbs High Protein

Main Recipes

Spinach Tomato Frittata

Servings : 4

23 grams Protein

15 grams Carb

17 grams Fat

280 Cal Per Serving

Est. Prep Time: 10 mins

Est. Cook Time: 15 mins

Est. Total Time: 25 mins

Ingredients

- 2 tbsp. olive oil
- 2 scallions, thinly sliced
- 10 oz. fresh baby spinach (or 10 oz pkg frozen chopped spinach, thawed and squeezed dry)
- 3 large eggs
- 5 large egg whites

- 1 c. grape or cherry tomatoes
- 4 slices fresh mozzarella
- 4 slices whole grain bread, toasted

Instructions

- In a large oven-safe, nonstick skillet, heat 1 tablespoon of the oil over medium heat. Scallions should be cooked for 1 minute while stirring to soften.
- Place the scallions in a big basin. Add egg whites, spinach, and whole eggs. Blend thoroughly by beating with a fork.
- Turn on the broiler. In a skillet, heat the remaining oil at medium-low heat. Add the egg mixture, then sprinkle the tomatoes on top. Cook the eggs for 4 minutes with the lid on, or until the edges are set.
- For 4 minutes, or until the frittata is gently browned and the center is set,

broil 5 inches from the flame. Cheese should be added on top, covered, and left to melt for one minute. Each wedge should be served with a slice of toast.

High-Protein Veggie Egg

Servings : 2

17 grams Protein

5 grams Carb

15 grams Fat

224 Cal Per Serving

Est. Prep Time: 10 mins

Est. Cook Time: 15 mins

Est. Total Time: 25 mins

Ingredients

- Cooking spray or ghee
- 3 cups low-carb chopped vegetables, such as kale, scallions, broccoli and peppers
- ½ cup water
- 4 ounces shredded sharp cheddar cheese, 1 cup, such as Cheddar

- 11 large eggs
- 2 teaspoons Dijon mustard
- 1 teaspoon smoked paprika, optional
- ½ teaspoon salt
- ¼ teaspoon ground pepper

Instructions

- Set oven to 350 degrees Fahrenheit. Cooking spray or Ghee should be liberally applied to a 12-cup muffin pan.
- Fill a medium saucepan with the vegetables and water. Put a cover on it and heat it up. 4 minutes to cook. Vegetables should be taken off the heat and drained in a sieve.
- The muffin tin wells should be evenly divided with the vegetables. Add cheddar cheese on top. In a big bowl, combine eggs, mustard, paprika, salt, and pepper. Through a fine mesh sieve, pour the egg

mixture into a large measuring cup. Pour carefully over the cheese and vegetables, distributing it equally among the cups.
- Place in the oven, and bake for 18 to 22 minutes, or until the eggs are puffy in the center. To remove from the pan, wait at least 20 minutes for it to cool. Refrigerate

Chicken in Air Fryer

Servings : 4

38.3 grams Protein

0 grams Carb

4.5 grams Fat

204 Cal Per Serving

Est. Prep Time: …mins

Est. Cook Time: 22 mins

Est. Total Time: 22 mins

Ingredients

- 4 boneless skinless chicken breasts
- black pepper (optional)
- Chicken marinade ingredients:
- ⅓ cup orange juice, freshly squeezed (from 1-2 oranges)
- 1 tablespoon lemon juice, fresh squeezed (from 1 lemon)
- 1 tablespoon lime juice, fresh squeezed (from 1 lime)

- 1 tablespoon orange zest
- ½ tablespoon lemon zest
- ½ tablespoon lime zest
- 1 tablespoon extra virgin olive oil
- 1 teaspoon cumin
- 3 cloves garlic, minced

Instructions

- Make the marinade for the chicken first. Orange, lemon, and lime should be juiced and zested. (Microplane and a manual juicer are useful tools here.)
- The crushed garlic cloves are combined with the juices, zest, cumin, and olive oil. The marinade is finished!
- Place your chicken breasts in a Ziploc bag or other food-safe container. Pour the marinade over the chicken to cover it. The chicken should marinate for 4 to 8

hours in the fridge. Seal the bag (or cover the container). Flip the chicken every few hours if the marinade is not completely covering it.
- For five minutes, heat the air fryer to 350°F (175°C).
- Place the chicken on the hot air fryer trays after discarding the marinade. Per tray, I could fit two chicken breasts.
- At 350°F (175°C), air fried the chicken that has been marinated for 12 minutes. After that, flip the chicken with a spatula and reposition the air fryer's trays. For an additional 8–10 minutes, air fry.
- A meat thermometer should be used to check the thickest area of the chicken breasts. Chicken must be cooked to a minimum internal temperature of 165°F (74°C). The air fryer may need to cook

some of the chicken pieces for a little while longer.

- Prior to serving, give the chicken about 10 minutes to rest. If desired, add a little black pepper as a garnish.

Shrimp, Avocado, and Egg Chopped Salad

Servings : 2

40 grams Protein

15 grams Carb

17 grams Fat

365 Cal Per Serving

Est. Prep Time: 10 mins

Est. Cook Time: 15 mins

Est. Total Time: 25 mins

Ingredients

- 1/4 small red onion, thinly sliced
- 2 tbsp. fresh lime juice
- 1 tbsp. olive oil
- 12 oz. large peeled and deveined shrimp
- Kosher salt and pepper
- 1 c. grape tomatoes, halved
- 8 c. butter lettuce

- 1/2 c. fresh cilantro leaves
- 1/2 avocado, diced
- 2 hard boiled eggs, cut into pieces

Instructions

- Mix the onion with the lime juice and 1/2 tablespoon oil in a big bowl, and set aside for 5 minutes.
- Put a big skillet on medium-high heat and add 1/2 tablespoon of oil. Add 1/4 teaspoon each of salt and pepper to the shrimp and cook for 2 to 3 minutes on each side, or until opaque throughout.
- Combine the lettuce and cilantro with the tomatoes and onions. Add shrimp, avocado, and eggs on top after dividing among dishes.

Rotisserie Chicken Salad Recipe

Servings : 4

21 grams Protein

14 grams Carb

20 grams Fat

305 Cal Per Serving

Est. Prep Time: 15 mins

Est. Cook Time: 3 mins

Est. Total Time: 18 mins

Ingredients

- 2 cups Leftover Rotisserie Chicken
- 1/4 cup Cooked Chickpeas
- 1 Avocado
- 12 Grape Tomatoes
- 1 Cucumber medium
- ¼ Small Onion
- 5 springs Dill
- 1 Lemon
- 2 tbsp Olive Oil

- 1 pinch Salt
- 1 pinch Ground Black Pepper

Instructions

- On a chopping board, clean and chop the avocado.
- Wash and peel the cucumber, dill, and grape tomatoes. Wash and peel the onion.
- Mince the dill, onions, and cucumber. Cut the grape tomatoes in half lengthwise.
- Using a lemon juicer, wash the lemon and extract its juice.
- To the salad dish, add the chicken, avocados, chickpeas, cucumbers, tomatoes, onions, and dill. Add a tablespoon of the lemon juice along with the olive oil. Salt and pepper the salad

after a gentle mixing. It's time to serve the salad.

Pan Seared Chicken Breast Recipe

Servings : 4

50 grams Protein

14 grams Carb

25 grams Fat

478 Cal Per Serving

Est. Prep Time: …mins

Est. Cook Time: …mins

Est. Total Time: …mins

Ingredients

- 28 oz skinless boneless chicken breast
- 0.3 tsp black pepper divided
- 0.5 tsp salt divided
- 0.3 tsp paprika
- 0.3 tsp oregano
- 0.3 tsp garlic powder
- 3 tbsp olive oil divided
- 2.8 tbsp unsalted butter
- 16 oz asparagus sliced

- 8 oz cremini mushrooms brown, medium-sliced
- 4 oz onion sliced
- 1 tsp garlic chopped
- 5 oz carrot
- 0.5 tsp Italian Seasoning
- 0.5 oz grated parmesan cheese
- 2 tbsp parsley fresh

Instructions

- Make vertical cuts along the chicken breast's surface with a sharp knife.
- Combine oregano, 1/8 teaspoon pepper, 1/4 teaspoon salt, paprika, and garlic powder in a small bowl. Add 1 tablespoon of olive oil next.
- Chicken breasts should be marinated in the spice-oil combination.

- Add 1 tbsp of olive oil to a non-stick skillet that is already hot over medium heat.
- Chicken breasts are added, and they are sautéed for about 8 minutes, until they are golden brown on both sides. Get rid of the heat.
- Before reheating it over medium heat, clean the pan. Add 1 tablespoon of olive oil. Golden brown mushrooms require 2 minutes of stir-frying.
- Garlic, onions, and carrots should all be chopped. Add asparagus after 2 minutes of stir-frying.
- Add the final 1/4 teaspoon of salt, 1/8 teaspoon of pepper, and Italian seasoning to taste. Then, after cooking the vegetables for about 6 minutes, add butter and turn off the heat.

- Add some parmesan cheese and fresh parsley before serving.

Salmon Meal Prep With Veggies (High Protein)

Servings : 2

54 grams Protein

40 grams Carb

45 grams Fat

806 Cal Per Serving

Est. Prep Time: ...mins

Est. Cook Time: ...mins

Est. Total Time: 30 mins

Ingredients

- 1 lb salmon (450g)
- 1/2 sweet potato (250g)
- 2 cups of cauliflower (200g)
- 2 tbsp olive oil
- 1 tbsp soy sauce
- ½ tsp garlic powder
- ½ tsp ground ginger
- ½ tsp cumin

- ½ tsp paprika
- 1 cup cooked and diced beets (120g)
- 4 lemon wedges
- Parsley
- salt and pepper, to taste

Instructions

- Set the oven to 400 degrees (200C). Combine ginger, garlic, and 1 tablespoon of olive oil. Spread the cauliflower out on the baking sheets after tossing it with the mixture.
- Combine cumin, paprika, and 1 tablespoon of olive oil. Sweet potatoes should be cut into cubes and then spread out on baking pans after being coated with the oil mixture. Stir halfway through a 25–30 minute roasting period in the oven.

- Put some salt and pepper on the salmon. The salmon should be fried for a minute with the skin on before adding soy sauce and another tablespoon of olive oil.
- After about one to two minutes, flip the salmon over so the skin is on. The salmon should then be cooked through after an additional 3-5 minutes of cooking.
- Slice the parsley and dice the beets. Divide the salmon and veggies among the glass jars, then top with the lemon wedges and fresh parsley.

Stir-Fried Pork Meal Prep With Ginger and Soy

Servings : 2

32 grams Protein

29 grams Carb

19 grams Fat

409 Cal Per Serving

Est. Prep Time: ...mins

Est. Cook Time: ...mins

Est. Total Time: 30 mins

Ingredients

- 9 oz pork tenderloin (250g), cut into chunks
- 1 tsp cornflour
- 2 tbsp dark soy sauce
- 2 tbsp olive oil
- 2.5 oz green beans (75g)
- 1 red pepper, deseeded and sliced
- 1 yellow pepper, deseeded and sliced

- 1 green pepper, deseeded and sliced
- 2.5 oz snow peas (75g)
- ½ oz fresh root ginger (75g), finely chopped
- 2 garlic cloves, minced
- 4 spring onions, cut into short lengths
- black pepper
- 2 tbsp of water

Instructions

- Remove all of the pork's fat by cutting the meat into bits. Combine 2 tbsp of cold water with the cornmeal.
- Heat up 1 tablespoon of olive oil in a frying pan before adding the pork. The meat should be gently browned but not totally cooked after 2 minutes of stirring.
- After taking the pork out of the pan, add one more tablespoon of olive oil. Peppers

should be sliced and added to the pan. Then include the green beans.
- After 2 minutes, stir in the snow peas. Stir-fry spring onions, ginger, and garlic.
- Return the pork to the frying pan and stir in the soy sauce and cornstarch water combination. Cook for a further 2 to 4 minutes, or until the sauce has thickened and the meat is thoroughly cooked.

Sheet Pan Italian Sausage and Pepper Bake

Servings : 4

16 grams Protein

10 grams Carb

13 grams Fat

210 Cal Per Serving

Est. Prep Time: …mins

Est. Cook Time: …mins

Est. Total Time: 30 mins

Ingredients

- 4 sweet or hot Italian turkey sausages (about 12 oz.), cut into 1 1/2-in. pieces
- 2 peppers (orange, red, or a combination), halved, seeded, and thickly sliced
- 1 pt. cherry or grape tomatoes, halved
- 1 medium yellow onion, cut into 1-in. wedges

- 1 clove garlic, finely chopped
- 1 tbsp. olive oil
- 1 tsp. dried oregano
- Kosher salt and pepper

Instructions

- 400°F oven temperature. Toss the sausages with the peppers, tomatoes, onions, and garlic on a large rimmed baking sheet along with the oil, oregano, 1/4 teaspoon salt, and 1/8 teaspoon pepper.
- Roast for 15 to 20 minutes, or until veggies are golden brown and soft and sausages are thoroughly cooked and starting to blister.

Chicken With Fried Cauliflower Rice

Servings : 4

34 grams Protein

18 grams Carb

13 grams Fat

340 Cal Per Serving

Est. Prep Time: 10 mins

Est. Cook Time: 25 mins

Est. Total Time: 35 mins

Ingredients

- 1 tbsp. plus 2 teaspoons grapeseed oil
- 1 lb. boneless, skinless chicken breast, pounded to even thickness
- 4 large eggs, beaten
- 2 red peppers, finely chopped
- 2 small carrots, finely chopped
- 1 small onion, finely chopped
- 2 cloves garlic, finely chopped

- 4 scallions, finely chopped, plus more for serving
- 1 c. frozen peas, thawed
- 4 c. cauliflower "rice"
- 2 tbsp. low-sodium soy sauce
- 2 tsp. rice vinegar
- Kosher salt and pepper

Instructions

- A sizable, deep skillet is warmed to medium-high heat. Cook the chicken in 1 tablespoon oil for 3 to 4 minutes on each side or until golden brown. Transfer the chicken to a cutting board and let it rest for 6 minutes before slicing.
- Scramble the eggs in the skillet with 2 teaspoons of oil until just set, 1 to 2 minutes, and then transfer to a bowl.

- Add the red pepper, carrot, and onion and cook, stirring frequently, for 4 to 5 minutes, or until just tender. Add the garlic and heat for one minute. Combine with peas and scallions.
- Combine the cauliflower, soy sauce, and rice vinegar. After that, leave the cauliflower alone for 2 to 3 minutes, or until it starts to become brown. Add sliced chicken and eggs before mixing.

Moroccan Eggs with Harissa Yogurt

Servings : 4

19.8 grams Protein

6.9 grams Carb

22.9 grams Fat

318 Cal Per Serving

Est. Prep Time: 10 mins

Est. Cook Time: 25 mins

Est. Total Time: 35 mins

Ingredients

- 1/2 teaspoon each: fennel seeds, cumin seeds, caraway seeds
- 1/2 onion, diced
- 4 garlic cloves, rough chopped
- 1 lb ground American lamb
- 1 teaspoon salt
- 2 teaspoons smoked paprika
- 2 teaspoons cumin

- 1/2 teaspoon aleppo chili flakes (or regular chili flakes)
- 1/2 teaspoon cinnamon
- 14-ounce can fire-roasted tomatoes (and juices) , diced
- 1/4 cup water, more as needed
- 2 cups chopped spinach (fresh, or use one cup frozen)
- 6 eggs
- salt and pepper to taste

Instructions

- Set the oven to 375°F.
- Toast the whole spices in a dry skillet over medium heat for 1-2 minutes, or until aromatic and brown. Place aside.
- Over medium heat, add the onion, garlic, and ground lamb to the skillet. Saute the mixture until the lamb is thoroughly

cooked (about 8 minutes) Add the salt, spices, and whole spices while it is sautéing. Ten minutes of low heat, covered simmering with the addition of the tomatoes, spinach, and water.
- Taste the stew and add more salt or spice as desired. Add a bit additional water if it appears dry to make it somewhat juicier and still warm.
- With the back of a spoon, create six "wells" in the stew, and then crack the eggs into each well. Place eggs in the oven after seasoning with salt and pepper.
- Bake for 7 to 10 minutes, or until the yolks are still soft but the whites are cooked through and opaque.
- Mix the yogurt with the harissa paste to serve alongside as this bakes (or spoon over top). view notes

- Add the cilantro and Aleppo to the garnish (or chili flakes).

Roasted Chicken and Potatoes With Kale

Servings : 4

38 grams Protein

29 grams Carb

29 grams Fat

526 Cal Per Serving

Est. Prep Time: 10 mins

Est. Cook Time: 25 mins

Est. Total Time: 35 mins

Ingredients

- 1 lb. yellow potatoes, cut into 3/4-in. pieces
- 1/2 c. green olives
- 2 tsp. fresh thyme leaves
- 3 tbsp. olive oil, divided
- kosher salt
- pepper
- 1 lemon, halved

- 1 tsp. paprika
- 4 small chicken legs, split (4 drumsticks and 4 thighs; about 2 1/2 lbs.)
- 4 c. baby kale

Instructions

- Toaster oven: 425 °F. Toss potatoes, olives, and thyme with 2 tablespoons oil, 1/4 teaspoon salt, and 1/4 teaspoon pepper on a large rimmed baking sheet. Place the cut edges of the lemon halves on the baking sheet.
- Combine the remaining tbsp. of oil, the paprika, and 1/2 tsp. of salt and pepper in a small bowl. Chicken is placed on a baking pan between veggies after being thoroughly coated with the mixture.

- Roast the veggies and chicken for 25 to 30 minutes, or until the chicken is golden brown and well cooked.
- Put the chicken on plates, add the kale to the pan with the veggies, and then put the pan back in the oven for about a minute, or until the kale starts to wilt. Potatoes with kale have been combined. Lemon juice has been drizzled over the vegetables.

White Wine and Tomato Mussels

Servings : 4

25 grams Protein

15 grams Carb

11.5 grams Fat

269 Cal Per Serving

Est. Prep Time: 10 mins

Est. Cook Time: 25 mins

Est. Total Time: 35 mins

Ingredients

- 2 tbsp. olive oil
- 2 large cloves garlic, finely chopped
- 1 red chile, finely chopped
- 1 c. dry white wine
- 1/4 tsp. kosher salt
- 2 lb. mussels, scrubbed and beards removed
- 2 medium tomatoes (about 1 lb. total), seeded and chopped

- 1/2 c. basil, chopped
- 1/2 c. parsley, chopped

Instructions

- Olive oil, garlic, and red chile are heated in a big Dutch oven for three minutes on medium-low. add white wine; boil for 2 minutes.
- Add kosher salt, then the mussels, and simmer for 4 minutes with the lid on and occasional tossing. Put the mussels in a small basin.
- 2 minutes after adding the tomatoes. Take off the heat, stir in the basil and parsley, and then spoon over the mussels.

Baked Salmon with Roasted Red Pepper Sauce

Servings : 3

35.7 grams Protein

8.2 grams Carb

20.6 grams Fat

351 Cal Per Serving

Est. Prep Time: 10 mins

Est. Cook Time: 25 mins

Est. Total Time: 35 mins

Ingredients

- 1/2 cup jarred roasted red peppers (see notes if using fresh peppers)
- 1/4 cup smoked nuts (almonds and/or cashews)
- 1 plum tomato, chopped
- 2 Tablespoon red wine vinegar or sherry cooking wine
- 1 clove of garlic

- Pinch of paprika
- 1/4 teaspoon crushed red pepper
- 1/3 cup or 3–4 ounces heavy cream (or non dairy unsweetened creamer/milk)
- Fine kosher salt and pepper to taste
- (printable sauce recipe can be found here)
- 3 fillets or 15–18 ounces of salmon, skin removed
- 1 Tablespoon coconut oil, ghee, or other high smoke point oil
- 1/2 lemon, cut into slices
- 1 Tablespoon fresh oregano
- Sea salt
- Black pepper

Instructions

- Blend every component of the sauce but the cream.
- Cream should be stirred into the sauce in a small saucepan over low heat. 2-4 minutes of low-heat stirring should result in warm, smooth, and blended results. Place aside.
- Set the oven at 400 F.
- In an oven-safe pan, heat the oil over medium-high heat.
- Salmon should be seared in heated oil for 2 minutes on one side before being turned over and seared for an additional 2 minutes.
- Fill the pan with fish and the prepared roasted pepper sauce. After two minutes of heating, place the pan in the oven.
- Salmon should be baked for 10 minutes at 400°F or until no longer pink.

- Lemon slices and oregano are garnishes. Add sea salt and pepper to taste when seasoning.

Roasted Shrimp Parmesan

Servings : 4

33 grams Protein

23 grams Carb

17.5 grams Fat

348 Cal Per Serving

Est. Prep Time: …mins

Est. Cook Time: 40 mins

Est. Total Time: 40 mins

Ingredients

- 3 tbsp. olive oil, divided
- 6 oz. rustic bread, torn into 3/4-in. pieces
- kosher salt
- pepper
- 2 cloves garlic, finely chopped
- 1 lb. plum tomatoes, cut into 1/2-in. pieces

- 1 small bunch basil, leaves torn, divided
- 1 lb. large shrimp, peeled and deveined
- 3 oz. mozzarella cheese, grated (about 1 c.)
- 3 tbsp. grated Parmesan cheese

Instructions

- 425°F oven temperature. In a big oven-safe skillet, heat 2 tablespoons of oil to medium-low. Add the bread and coat with oil before seasoning with 1/4 tsp of salt and pepper. Bake the bread in the skillet for 8 to 10 minutes, or until it is crisp and golden brown.
- Place the remaining tablespoon of oil and garlic in the skillet after removing bread to a plate. About 1 minute, while stirring,

cook garlic until it starts to turn golden brown. Add tomatoes and 1/4 teaspoon of salt and pepper, and simmer, stirring periodically, for 5 to 7 minutes, or until tomatoes start to release juices. Fold in the basil in half.

- Add bread and prawns to the tomato mixture.
- Bake for 14 to 16 minutes, or until the cheese is golden brown and bubbling, and the shrimp are opaque throughout. Serve right away with the remaining basil sprinkled on top.

Honey Lime Air Fryer Shrimp

Servings : 4

23 grams Protein

7 grams Carb

7 grams Fat

187 Cal Per Serving

Est. Prep Time: …mins

Est. Cook Time: 40 mins

Est. Total Time: 40 mins

Ingredients

- 1 lb large shrimp raw; remove shell and tail if desired; note 1
- 1 ½ tablespoons olive oil
- 1 ½ tablespoons lime juice note 2
- 1 ½ tablespoons honey note 3
- 2 cloves garlic minced
- ⅛ teaspoon salt
- lime wedges
- cilantro

Instructions

- To make the marinade, combine the olive oil, lime juice, honey, garlic, and salt in a big bowl. For 20 to 30 minutes, add the shrimp and marinate.
- Heat the air fryer to 390°F/200°C to prepare food.
- Shake off any extra marinade from the shrimp before placing the entire batch in the air fryer.
- Cook for 2 minutes, then return to the air fryer after giving the basket a good shake. Cook the shrimp for a further 2 to 3 minutes, or until pink and fully cooked.
- Serve with cilantro and lime wedges.

Baked Chicken Nuggets

Servings : 4

43 grams Protein

6 grams Carb

16 grams Fat

339 Cal Per Serving

Est. Prep Time: …mins

Est. Cook Time: …mins

Est. Total Time: …mins

Ingredients

- 1.5 lb organic boneless skinless chicken breast, cut into chunks/nuggets
- ½ cup dill pickle juice
- 1 egg
- 1 cup almond flour
- 1 teaspoon garlic powder
- 1/2 teaspoon paprika
- 1 teaspoon sea salt

- 1/2 teaspoon black pepper

Instructions

- In pickle juice, marinate chicken for 8 to 12 hours.
- Set the oven to 425 °F.
- In a small bowl, combine the almond flour, paprika, garlic, sea salt, and black pepper. To blend, stir.
- In a different small bowl, crack an egg, and whisk it.
- Each chicken nugget should be coated individually in the egg mixture, wiped of any excess, and then dipped into the almond flour mixture. Roll each nugget until it is entirely covered. Put the coated nuggets on a wire rack that may fit on a baking sheet or a baking pan that has been lined with parchment paper. The texture will be crispier thanks to the wire

rack. The nuggets should be baked for 20 to 30 minutes, flipping them once after 10 minutes.
- In pickle juice, marinate chicken for 8 to 12 hours. Preheat
- The finished chicken nuggets should be crisp, golden brown, and fully cooked. Before serving, take the nuggets out of the oven and let them cool somewhat.

Beef and Broccoli

Servings : 4

28 grams Protein

10 grams Carb

16 grams Fat

305 Cal Per Serving

Est. Prep Time: …mins

Est. Cook Time: …mins

Est. Total Time: …mins

Ingredients

- 1/3 cup Coconut aminos
- 1 tbsp Fish sauce
- 1 tsp Ground ginger
- 1/4 tsp Crushed red pepper
- 1 tbsp Olive oil
- 1/4 cup Chicken broth, reduced sodium
- 1 tbsp Unflavored gelatin powder
- 2 tbsp Olive oil (divided)

- 4 cups Broccoli (cut into florets)
- 2 cloves Garlic (minced)
- 1 lb Flank steak (sliced as thinly as possible)

Instructions

- Mix the coconut aminos, fish sauce, ground ginger, and red pepper flakes in a small bowl.
- To make the marinade, pour 2 teaspoons (30 mL) of the coconut aminos mixture into a large basin. One tablespoon of olive oil is whisked in.
- The steak should be added to the large bowl of marinade and coated. 30 minutes should be spent cooling.
- In a saute pan or wok, heat one tablespoon (15 mL) of olive oil over high heat. Stir-fry the beef for a few minutes, or until it has browned. The beef should

be taken out, put in a basin, and covered to keep warm.

- Over medium heat, warm up one more tablespoon of olive oil. the broccoli, please.
- Cook the food for 8 to 12 minutes, stirring slightly occasionally, until it is crisp and tender.
- Broccoli is removed, added to the bowl containing the beef, and covered once more to maintain warmth.
- In the smaller bowl, stir the reserved marinade/sauce and chicken broth until well combined. (To avoid clumping, sprinkle the gelatin over it rather than pouring it in.) Then, stir right away.
- Reheat the pan on a medium heat setting. More oil should be added if the pan is dry. When aromatic, add the garlic and sauté for about a minute.

- The sauce mixture should be poured into the pan and simmered.
- For about 5 minutes, simmer, stirring now and again, until volume is reduced and it begins to thicken.
- Toss the steak and broccoli in the pan with the sauce. Stir-fry for a further one or two minutes, or until heated.

Slow Cooker Beef Chile Verde

Servings : 10

25.5 grams Protein

4.6 grams Carb

4.8 grams Fat

163 Cal Per Serving

Est. Prep Time: …mins

Est. Cook Time: …mins

Est. Total Time: …mins

Ingredients

- 2-3 pounds beef chuck
- 1 jar (12-16 oz) salsa verde or green enchilada sauce (try homemade or FODY Foods for low FODMAP)
- 1 can green chiles
- Salt & pepper - about ½ teaspoon of each
- Optional: 1 medium onion, sliced into wedges, 4 cloves minced garlic

- For serving: Mexican quick-pickled spicy carrots, sliced avocado, fresh cilantro, tortilla chips (I like Siete), cauliflower rice, limes

Instructions

- Place the beef chuck in the slow cooker after seasoning it with salt and pepper all over.
- If using, cut the onions into wedges and place them in the slow cooker with the beef. Also add the minced garlic.
- The salsa verde or green enchilada sauce and the diced green chilis should be added to the slow cooker and distributed equally over the beef and onions.
- Until the meat is extremely soft, cook covered over LOW heat for 8–12 hours.
- With two forks, shred the beef and serve it plain or in a variety of other ways, such

as in quesadillas, tacos, on nachos, or with eggs for breakfast!

Salsa Shredded Chicken

Servings : 2

62 grams Protein

46 grams Carb

16 grams Fat

554 Cal Per Serving

Est. Prep Time: …mins

Est. Cook Time: …mins

Est. Total Time: …mins

Ingredients

- 3 boneless, skinless chicken breasts (1lb, 450g)
- 16 oz mild salsa sauce (450g)
- 1/2 cup chicken broth
- 1 tsp chili powder
- 1 tsp paprika powder
- 1 lb cauliflower floret (450g)
- ½ tsp salt
- 1 red bell pepper

- 1 yellow bell pepper
- 1 green bell pepper
- 1 tbsp olive oil
- Pinch of salt

Instructions

- Chicken breasts should be removed and placed in a pot. Add the salsa sauce and chicken broth. Add chili powder and paprika. Stir it around.
- Put a lid on the pot and heat it until it boils. Reduce the heat after that and simmer the mixture for 30 minutes.
- Set the oven to 425 degrees (220 C). All of the bell peppers should be cut into 12 inch (1.3 cm) wide strips. Then, spread some olive oil on them and arrange them on a baking pan. Sprinkle some salt on top and make sure the peppers are completely covered. After that, roast for

20 to 25 minutes, or until just beginning to brown.
- Take out the cauliflower floret while the chicken is boiling and the peppers are baking. Wash it and disassemble it. It should be shred in a food processor after about ten minutes of steaming. Once finished, season to your taste with some salt.
- After the chicken has simmered for 30 minutes, shred it inside the saucepan with forks, then give it a stir. Cut the heat off.
- Add salt to the cauliflower and place it in the food storage containers when all of the cooking is finished. Divide each serving in half, then put chicken in the container with roasted peppers.
- This meal preparation can be kept in the refrigerator for up to 4 days. The food

tends to stay fresher longer in glass containers.

Egg Salad Bowls

Servings : 2

27 grams Protein

13 grams Carb

31 grams Fat

469 Cal Per Serving

Est. Prep Time: ...mins

Est. Cook Time: ...mins

Est. Total Time: ...mins

Ingredients

- 6 hard-boiled eggs
- 1/3 cup plain non-fat Greek yogurt
- 2 tsp dijon mustard
- 3 celery stalks (chopped)
- ½ tsp lemon zest
- 1 tsp fresh lemon juice
- 1 tbsp parsley (chopped)
- 1 tbsp dill
- 1/2 tsp salt

- 1/4 tsp black pepper
- 9 oz cherry tomatoes (250g) (halved)
- 0.5 red onion (sliced)
- 1 avocado (sliced)

Instructions

- For 10 minutes, boil the eggs in water.
- Chop the eggs after peeling them.
- Lemon zest, dijon mustard, Greek yogurt, salt, and black pepper should all be combined. Stir in chopped celery, parsley, and dill.
- Stir the dressing after adding the chopped eggs.
- Slice an onion, an avocado, and a tomato.
- Put the vegetables in each food container separately. Add the egg salad after that.
- Fresh lemon juice should be drizzled atop the avocado. That will prevent it from rusting.

- Keep in the fridge for up to 3 to 4 days.

Mexican Meal Prep Bowls with Cauliflower Rice

Servings : 4

48 grams Protein

9 grams Carb

17 grams Fat

406 Cal Per Serving

Est. Prep Time: ...mins

Est. Cook Time: ...mins

Est. Total Time: ...mins

Ingredients

- 1 head cauliflower
- 1 tbsp olive oil
- 1 green bell pepper (chopped)
- 1 can chopped tomatoes (1.5 cup chopped tomatoes)
- 1 tsp ground onion
- 1/2 tsp garlic powder
- 1/2 tsp cumin

- 1 tsp paprika
- 1/4 tsp crushed chili flakes
- 1/2 tsp dried oregano
- pinch of salt
- pinch of black pepper
- 4 boneless, skinless chicken breasts
- ½ tsp salt
- ¼ tsp black pepper
- 1 cup wild rocket salad
- 1 avocado

Instructions

- Chicken breasts should be placed in a big saucepan along with salt and pepper.
- Around 1 inch of water should be spread over the bird.
- The water should be brought to a boil before simmering for around 12 minutes. Take the chicken out of the water, then

shred it with a fork, a pair of claws, or a food processor.
- Dissect the cauliflower head. Cleaning, drying, and cutting into smaller pieces.
- Use a food processor to pulse until cauliflower rice is produced.
- Green pepper should be chopped, added to a hot skillet with olive oil, and sautéed for a few minutes.
- Cook the cauliflower rice and chopped tomatoes for five minutes.

Turkey Kebabs

Servings : 4

22 grams Protein

3 grams Carb

8 grams Fat

158 Cal Per Serving

Est. Prep Time: …mins

Est. Cook Time: …mins

Est. Total Time: …mins

Ingredients

- 400 g Turkey breast - cut into chunks
- 2 tablespoon Olive oil
- 2 pinch Sea salt and black pepper
- 1 teaspoon paprika
- 0.5 teaspoon Ground turmeric
- 0.5 teaspoon ground cumin
- 3 Garlic clove - crushed
- 0.5 Lemon - juice only
- 5 g Fresh parsley - finely chopped

Instructions

- Combine the oil, seasonings, parsley, garlic, and lemon juice in a bowl.
- Place the marinade and turkey chunks in a bowl. Mix thoroughly, then chill for at least two hours.
- Glue the skewers with the pre-soaked turkey marinade onto them. 10 minutes of grilling while rotating frequently.

Broiled Beef Shish Kebabs

Servings : 4

92 grams Protein

3 grams Carb

49 grams Fat

938 Cal Per Serving

Est. Prep Time: …mins

Est. Cook Time: …mins

Est. Total Time: …mins

Ingredients

- 3 lbs. Top Sirloin Steak diced into large 2 inch pieces
- 1/4 cup Fresh parsley chopped
- ½ Yellow onion quartered and pieces separated
- 2 cups Red Wine
- 2 tsp. Salt
- 2 tsp. Black Pepper
- 1 tsp. Aleppo Pepper optional

Instructions

- Start by cutting the steak's fat. Slice the meat crosswise into 2 inch-long slices.
- Insert the fragments in a mixing bowl. Add a lot of salt, black pepper, and, if using, Aleppo pepper to the dish. Along with the onion quarters, add the chopped parsley.
- Mix well after adding the red wine. Allow it to marinate for at least a couple of hours under plastic wrap (longer if possible).
- Set your oven's broiler to high temperature. Verify that the oven rack is set as high as it can be while still allowing space for the baking sheet to fit.
- To raise the kabobs, line a baking sheet with foil and set a cooling rack or roasting rack on top.

- 3 to 4 minutes on each side (this cooking time will vary depending on how rare you like your meat). Please be aware that every oven is unique. The meat should sear, but not become very dry.
- To allow the other side to cook as well, flip the kabobs halfway through cooking. For medium rare, cook at 125–130 F. If you prefer your steak more done, keep cooking as necessary.
- After taking them out of the oven, let them cool for five minutes. Serve the steak with your preferred sides after removing it from the skewers

Air Fryer Chicken Drumsticks

Servings : 3

27 grams Protein

2 grams Carb

19 grams Fat

290 Cal Per Serving

Est. Prep Time: 6 mins

Est. Cook Time: 19 mins

Est. Total Time: 25 mins

Ingredients

- 6 chicken drumsticks, skin-on
- 1 tablespoon oil, like vegetable or avocado oil
- 1 teaspoon salt
- ½ teaspoon freshly ground black pepper
- 1 teaspoon garlic powder
- 1 teaspoon paprika
- 1 teaspoon Italian seasoning

Instructions

- heating element to 400 degrees Fahrenheit.
- Fill a plastic storage bag that can hold a gallon with the chicken and the oil. Till the chicken is totally covered in oil, move the chicken about inside the bag.
- Mix the herbs and spices together in a small basin. Shake the bag until the drumsticks are thoroughly coated after adding the mixture, sealing it, and shaking.
- Cook the drumsticks for 10 minutes in the air fryer basket. When the chicken achieves an internal temperature of 165 degrees F when measured in the meatiest part of the drumstick, turn the pieces over and cook for an additional 9 to 10 minutes.

- Prior to serving, let the food cool for five minutes.

Spinach Egg Bake

Servings : 6

19 grams Protein

3 grams Carb

17 grams Fat

245 Cal Per Serving

Est. Prep Time: 15 mins

Est. Cook Time: 45 mins

Est. Total Time: 60 mins

Ingredients

- 1 10- ounce block frozen chopped spinach, thawed
- 12 large eggs
- 2 cloves garlic, minced or grated on a microplane grater
- ¼ cup half and half
- 2 teaspoons Dijon mustard
- 1 teaspoon smoked paprika, optional
- ¾ teaspoon salt

- ¼ teaspoon ground black or white pepper
- Pinch nutmeg
- 4 ounces cheddar cheese, 1 cup

Instructions

- Set the oven to 350 degrees Fahrenheit. Spray cooking oil on a deep dish pie plate.
- Squeeze the extra moisture out of the spinach. Add the spinach to the pie plate that has been prepared.
- In a big bowl, combine eggs, garlic, and half and half. Salt, pepper, nutmeg, mustard, paprika (if used), and mix until all ingredients are well-combined and there are no noticeable mustard clumps. Over the spinach, pour the egg mixture. Add cheddar on top.

- Transfer the mixture carefully to the oven, and bake for about 45 minutes, or until the middle is set. Before slicing into wedges and serving, take the dish out of the oven and let it cool for at least 10 minutes. Alternately, let food cool fully, slice, and keep refrigerated for up to 5 days.

Air Fryer Cod

Servings : 3

26.7 grams Protein

0 grams Carb

6 grams Fat

160 Cal Per Serving

Est. Prep Time: 15 mins

Est. Cook Time: 45 mins

Est. Total Time: 60 mins

Ingredients

- 1 lb frozen cod 454 grams; three ½-inch (1.27 cm) thick fillets
- 1 tablespoon olive oil (divided)
- salt and pepper, to taste
- 1 recipe cod topping

Instructions

- On the air frying tray or in the air fryer basket, arrange the frozen cod pieces in a single layer.
- 350°F (175°C) air frying the cod for 4 minutes. (If your oven is equipped with an air fryer, use the top rack position.) After flipping the cod, add a 1/2 tablespoon of oil to the tops of the fillets. 7 minutes of air frying at 375°F (190°C).
- Once more turned over, brush the tops of the fish with the remaining oil (12 tbsp). 7-8 more minutes of air frying at 375°F (190°C).
- Make sure the cod has reached a minimum safe internal temperature of 145°F (63°C) by using a meat thermometer. Add more cooking time if necessary. If desired, season the fish with salt and pepper.

Salmon Croquette

Servings : 4

41 grams Protein

15 grams Carb

24 grams Fat

453 Cal Per Serving

Est. Prep Time: 15 mins

Est. Cook Time: 10 mins

Est. Total Time: 25 mins

Ingredients

- 24 oz skinless boneless salmon roughly chopped
- 0.5 tsp salt
- 0.3 tsp ground black pepper
- 1.5 medium egg beaten
- 0.5 oz scallion finely chopped
- 0.5 oz coriander finely chopped
- 0.5 oz parsley finely chopped
- 4 tsp traditional Dijon mustard

- 6 tbsp plain panko breadcrumbs ¼ cup + 2 tbsp
- 1 tsp paprika
- 2 tsp coriander powder
- 2 tsp garlic powder
- 1.5 tsp lemon juice divide into 1 tsp and ½ tsp
- 2 tbsp unsalted butter
- 0.3 cup sour cream
- 0.5 tsp garlic minced
- 1 tbsp balsamic vinegar
- 1 tbsp olive oil
- 1 teaspoon honey
- 1 oz radish thinly sliced
- 6 oz cherry tomatoes cut in half
- 4 oz romaine lettuce chopped
- 1 oz cashew roasted

Instructions

- Salmon should be chopped before being processed into a fine powder. Two pulses are sufficient. Rather than being smoothly mixed, the salmon should be quite lumpy. Place in a large bowl.
- a photo taken from above of mashed fish in a food processor.
- Add herbs and spices: Salt, black pepper, beaten egg, scallion, coriander, parsley, Dijon mustard, breadcrumbs, paprika, coriander powder, garlic powder, and 1 teaspoon of lemon juice should all be added to the salmon bowl. To evenly combine everything, use a spoon.
- Salmon that has been mashed and is combined with bread crumbs, egg wash, and additional herbs and spices.
- Making the patties Eight equal pieces of the salmon mixture should be made.

- Make thick, rounded patties out of each half by rolling it into a ball in your palms. Transfer to a dish, then reserve.
- a plastic gloved hand with a ball of salmon mixture in the palm.
- Patty preparation: Over low heat, add butter to a nonstick skillet. When the butter has melted, add the patties and cook for 8 minutes, rotating halfway through, until golden brown on both sides. Transfer cooked patties to a platter and reserve.
- an image of a black skillet with four salmon croquettes.
- Making the salmon's sauce: Sour cream, minced garlic, and the final 1/2 tsp of lemon juice should all be combined in a small bowl. Mix thoroughly and reserve.

- a depiction of a tiny bowl containing lemon juice, minced garlic, and sour cream.
- Making the salad dressing: Balsamic vinegar, olive oil, and honey should all be combined in a separate small bowl. Once the sauce is well-combined, whisk to emulsify it and set it aside.
- a depiction of a tiny bowl with honey, balsamic vinegar, and olive oil within.
- assemble the salad: Combine lettuce, tomatoes, radish, and cashews gently. On one side of the serving platter, arrange the salad. Over the salad, drizzle the dressing.
- A beautiful salad in a glass bowl that includes lettuce, tomato halves, radish slices, and cashews.

- Serve and plate: Spread the sauce over the salmon croquettes in the center of the plate before serving.

Lamb Shish Kebab

Servings : 4

92 grams Protein

3 grams Carb

49 grams Fat

938 Cal Per Serving

Est. Prep Time: 5 mins

Est. Cook Time: 15 mins

Est. Total Time: 20 mins

Ingredients

- 800 g Leg of lamb - cut into 4 cm/1.5in chunks
- 2 tablespoon Olive oil
- 3 tablespoon Plain yogurt
- 3 Garlic clove - crushed
- 0.5 Lemon - juice only
- 2 Bell peppers - cut into chunks
- 0.5 teaspoon Ground coriander
- 0.5 teaspoon Cumin

- 0.5 teaspoon cayenne pepper
- 0.5 teaspoon paprika
- 1 pinch Sea salt and black pepper
- 10 g Fresh parsley - finely chopped

Instructions

- In a bowl, combine all the ingredients (apart from the bell peppers). Place the bowl in the refrigerator for at least an hour, and preferably overnight.
- Mix well. Place the bowl in the refrigerator for at least an hour, and preferably overnight.
- The skewers will be threaded with peppers and seasoned lamb.
- Place in front of a hot grill for 15 minutes, flipping once. Serve warm.

Greek Sheet Pan Chicken

Servings : 4

29 grams Protein

15 grams Carb

12 grams Fat

284 Cal Per Serving

Est. Prep Time: 15 mins

Est. Cook Time: 20 mins

Est. Total Time: 35 mins

Ingredients

- 1 lb chicken breasts (diced)
- 1 red pepper (diced)
- 1 green pepper (diced)
- 1 yellow pepper (diced)
- 1 zucchini (sliced)
- 1 red onion (sliced)
- 2 tbsp olive oil
- 2 tbsp fresh lemon juice
- 6 cloves garlic (minced)

- 1 tbsp dried oregano
- 1 tbsp dried parsley
- 1/2 tsp salt
- 1/4 tsp black pepper
- 1/4 cup feta cheese (crumbled)

Instructions

- set the oven to 400 degrees.
- In a sizable sheet pan, add the chicken and the vegetables. Olive oil, lemon juice, garlic, oregano, dried parsley, salt, and black pepper are added over top.
- After thoroughly combining all the ingredients, bake the chicken for 20 minutes to achieve complete doneness.
- Before serving, take the dish out of the oven and top with feta cheese crumbles.

Low Carb Greek Chicken

Servings : 4

28 grams Protein

7 grams Carb

15 grams Fat

287 Cal Per Serving

Est. Prep Time: 15 mins

Est. Cook Time: 20 mins

Est. Total Time: 35 mins

Ingredients

- 1 lb Chicken breast (~3 cups after cooking)
- 1 1/2 tsp Sea salt (divided, plus more for brine)
- 3 tbsp Olive oil (divided into 1 tbsp and 2 tbsp)
- 1 tbsp Balsamic vinegar (optional)
- 1/2 tsp Black pepper (divided)

- 10 oz Zucchini (sliced into thin half moons, 1/4 inch thick, ~2.5 cups)
- 1/2 lb Grape tomatoes (halved, ~1 cup)
- 1/2 large Onion (cut into medium half moons, ~3/4 cup)
- 1/2 tbsp Dried dill
- 1/2 tbsp Dried parsley
- 1 tsp Dried oregano
- 1 tsp Garlic powder
- 1/4 cup Feta cheese (crumbled, optional - only if not dairy free, paleo or whole30)

Instructions

- Set the oven to 400 degrees Fahrenheit. Foil a very large sheet pan, then grease it generously.

- Add water to a big dish. Stir with 2 tablespoons of sea salt to dissolve. Place the chicken in the brine and let it sit for 10 to 20 minutes.
- Cut the zucchini, grape tomatoes, and onions as you wait.
- Combine the dried dill, parsley, oregano, and garlic powder in a small basin.
- When the chicken has finished brining, pat it dry and arrange the pieces on a baking sheet in a single row, near to one another but not touching.
- Brush the chicken with 1 tablespoon of olive oil on each side. To season the chicken, use 1/4 tsp of black pepper and 3/4 tsp sea salt.
- Use half of the herb mixture and sprinkle it on both sides.
- In the meantime, combine the chopped veggies with the remaining 2 tablespoons

of olive oil in a large bowl. Add the rest of the herb mixture together with the remaining 1/4 tsp of black pepper and 3/4 tsp sea salt. Stir thoroughly by tossing. On the baking sheet, arrange the vegetables in a single layer, taking care not to place them on top of the chicken.

- Drizzle the chicken and vegetables with the optional balsamic vinegar if you're using it. (You could alternatively combine part of it with the vegetables and pour the remaining sauce over the chicken.)
- For about 20 minutes, roast the chicken and vegetables in the oven, or until the vegetables are tender and the chicken is thoroughly cooked. After removing the pan from the oven, it should rest for 5 minutes.
- Transfer the chicken slices into containers for supper preparation. the

remaining space with vegetables. If you don't avoid dairy, add some feta cheese.

Instant Pot Salmon with Frozen Fillets

Servings : 4

44.4 grams Protein

3 grams Carb

6 grams Fat

315 Cal Per Serving

Est. Prep Time: 5 mins

Est. Cook Time: 10 mins

Est. Total Time: 15mins

Ingredients

- 12 ounces salmon fillets 6 ounces each, thawed or frozen
- 1 tablespoon ghee or butter
- ½ teaspoon sea salt
- 1 dash ground black pepper or to taste
- 1 medium lemon

Instructions

- Insert the trivet rack and 1 cup of water into the Instant Pot.
- Salmon fillets should be placed skin side down on a rack. Put ghee on the tops. Add salt and pepper to taste. Lemon slices are placed on top of each fillet.
- Make sure the valve is set to "Sealing" and lock the lid. Depending on whether the fillets are frozen or thawed, set the pressure cooker to manual high for 3 or 6 minutes.
- Open the valve to vent once the pressure cooking period is finished for a quick pressure release. Take the salmon out of the pot and garnish with the remaining lemon.

Protein Snack Pack

Servings : 5

34 grams Protein

28 grams Carb

40 grams Fat

589 Cal Per Serving

Est. Prep Time: …mins

Est. Cook Time: …mins

Est. Total Time: …mins

Ingredients

- 1 1/4 cups hummus
- 1 1/4 cups mixed nuts
- 2 cups cheddar cheese - chopped into cubes
- 12 ounces deli lunch meat
- 2 1/2 cups cherry tomatoes
- 2 1/2 cups sugar snap peas
- 1 large English cucumber - sliced
- 5 eggs - hard boiled

Instructions

- Put hummus in five small plastic cups with lids and close them (each will have approximately 2 ounces). Your favorite kind of nut or nut mixture should be placed in five additional plastic cups with lids and sealed with the lid. Place aside.
- In five single compartment containers, distribute the remaining ingredients: cheddar cheese, lunch meat, cherry tomatoes, sugar snap peas, English cucumber, and egg.
- Put one cup of hummus and one cup of nuts in each container. For up to 5 days, seal and place in the refrigerator. Enjoy!

Protein Pancakes

Servings : 2

32 grams Protein

3 grams Carb

21 grams Fat

337 Cal Per Serving

Est. Prep Time: 10mins

Est. Cook Time: 15mins

Est. Total Time: 25 mins

Ingredients

- 2 large eggs beaten
- 2 scoops unflavored whey protein powder use a zero carb whey protein isolate (60 grams)
- ⅓ cup heavy whipping cream
- 2 tablespoons Swerve confectioners sugar substitute
- 1 teaspoon baking powder
- 1 teaspoon vanilla extract

- ½ teaspoon cinnamon
- pinch nutmeg

Instructions

- The eggs and protein powder should be combined in a sizable mixing dish.
- Add cinnamon, vanilla, baking powder, and sugar replacement after whisking.
- Heavy whipping cream should be added to the mixture and whisked in. When the mixture resembles standard pancake batter in consistency, add extra water if it is too thick. Add a tiny bit of xanthan gum if it is too thin.
- Use greased pancake or egg rings to create circles with precise edges. A little of the batter should be added to a skillet that is already hot over medium heat. Cook on one side for about a minute

before flipping to cook the other. Apply the remaining batter in a similar manner.
- Choose your preferred keto-friendly toppings before serving.

Protein Waffles

Servings : 5

21 grams Protein

19 grams Carb

7 grams Fat

218 Cal Per Serving

Est. Prep Time: 10mins

Est. Cook Time: 15mins

Est. Total Time: 25 mins

Ingredients

- 4 eggs large
- 2/3 cup plain Greek yogurt I used full fat
- 1/4 cup any milk I used almond milk
- 1 cup oat flour
- 2 scoops (68g) plant based protein powder vanilla

Instructions

- Warm up the waffle maker. Whisk milk, yogurt, and eggs in a sizable mixing dish. Whisk in the protein powder and oat flour until thoroughly incorporated.
- Follow the instructions on your waffle maker to make waffles. Your waffle maker's size will determine the amount of batter needed. For each waffle, I use a large ice cream scoop of batter.
- Waffles should be cooked for 4-5 minutes or until golden and crispy.
- With your preferred waffle toppings, serve hot.

Volume Conversions

Cup	Ounce	Milliliter	TableSpoon
8 Cup	64 oz	1895 ml	128
6 Cup	48 oz	1420 ml	96
5 Cup	40 oz	1180 ml	80
4 Cup	32 oz	960 ml	64
2 Cup	16 oz	480 ml	32
1 Cup	8 oz	240 ml	16
¾ Cup	6 oz	177 ml	12
⅔ Cup	5 oz	158 ml	11
½ Cup	4 oz	118ml	8
⅜ Cup	3 oz	90 ml	6
⅓ Cup	2.5 oz	79 ml	5.5

¼ Cup	2 oz	59 ml	4
⅛ Cup	1 oz	30 ml	3
1/16 Cup	½ oz	15 ml	1

Fahrenheit	Celsius
100	37
150	65
200	93
250	121
300	150
325	160
350	180
375	190
400	200
435	220
450	230
500	260
525	274
550	288

Weight Conversion

Imperial	Metric
½oz	15g
1oz	29g
2oz	57g
3oz	85g
4oz	113g
5oz	141g
6oz	170g
8oz	227g
10oz	283g
12oz	340g
13oz	369g

14oz	397g
15oz	425g
1lb	453g

1 tablespoon = 3 teaspoons = 15 milliliters

4 tablespoons = 1/4 cup = 60 milliliters

1 ounce = 2 tablespoons = 30 milliliters

1 cup = 8 oz. = 250 milliliters

1 pint = 2 cups = 500 milliliters

1 quart = 4 cups = 950 milliliters

1 quart = 2 pints = 950 milliliters

1 gallon = 4 quarts = 3800 milliliters = 3.8 liters

Printed in Great Britain
by Amazon